A Sense of Science
Exploring Health

Claire Llewellyn

SEA-TO-SEA

Mankato Collingwood London

This edition first published in 2009 by
Sea-to-Sea Publications
Distributed by Black Rabbit Books
P.O. Box 3263
Mankato, Minnesota 56002

Printed in USA, North Mankato, MN

Library of Congress
Cataloging-in-Publication Data:

Llewellyn, Claire.
  Exploring health / Claire Llewellyn.
    p. cm. -- (A sense of science)
  Includes index.
  Summary: "A simple exploration of health that covers
nutrition, exercise, avoiding germs, and getting enough
sleep. Includes activities"--Provided by publisher.
  ISBN 978-1-59771-129-6
  1. Health--Juvenile literature. I. Title.
  RA777.L538 2009
  613--dc22
                              2008007329

9 8 7 6 5 4 3

Published by arrangement with
the Watts Publishing Group
Ltd, London.

November 2012
RD/711296/002

Editor: Jeremy Smith
Art Director: Jonathan Hair
Design: Matthew Lilly
Cover and design concept:
Jonathan Hair

Photograph credits:
Steve Shott except: Alamy: 15b,
21b, 22, 23b. Corbis: 19.
istockphoto: 6, 12, 13, 15t, 25.

Contents

Health is good!

It's good
to be healthy.

When we are healthy,
we have lots of energy.

We can think hard.

Skipping
How many times can you skip rope in one minute? Now try and beat your score.

We have a good appetite!

Food and health

The food we eat helps us stay healthy.

Egg

Cheese

Meat

Some foods help our body grow.

Some foods give us energy.

Rice

Potato

Bread

Taste it

Close your eyes and ask a friend to feed you different kinds of fruit. Can you tell what each one is?

Some foods help us fight sickness.

Fruit

Vegetables

Eating well

To be healthy, we need to eat many different kinds of food.

Every day, we need to eat five portions of fruit and vegetables. There are many different types of these.

Try not to eat too much sugary food.

Water is good for your body. It is much better for you than sugary drinks.

Glug, glug
Measure how much water you drink every day. Would it fill a glass, a pitcher, or a bucket?

Exercise

Exercise helps us to stay healthy.

When we work our body, we make it stronger.

In and out

When we breathe, we use our lungs. Take a deep breath in and out. Which parts of your body move?

Running around is good for our muscles and bones.

Exercise is good for our heart and lungs.

Keep active!

We can exercise our body in all sorts of ways.

J-J-J-Jump!
Jump up and down for a minute. Stop. What changes do you notice in your body?

We can walk instead of ride in a car.

We can play
outside instead of
watch TV.

It's fun to be active with friends.

All about germs

Germs are tiny things that live on our bodies. Some of them can make us sick.

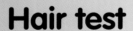

Hair test

Examine your hair before and after washing. What do you notice about the way it looks and feels?

To stay healthy, we need to wash them away!

We can brush away the germs that can rot our teeth.

Wash cuts and cover them to keep germs out.

Stop germs spreading

Germs can spread easily and make lots of people sick.

Soap song
It takes time to wash your hands well. Sing the whole verse of "Happy Birthday" while you rub them with soap.

Stop germs from spreading by washing your hands when you have been to the bathroom.

Catch germs in a paper tissue when you sneeze.

Wash your hands after touching a pet.

Germs and food

Some germs can spoil our food.

Bad food tastes awful and can make us sick.

Nice or nasty?

Put a piece of bread in a plastic bag and leave it somewhere warm for a few days. What happens to it?

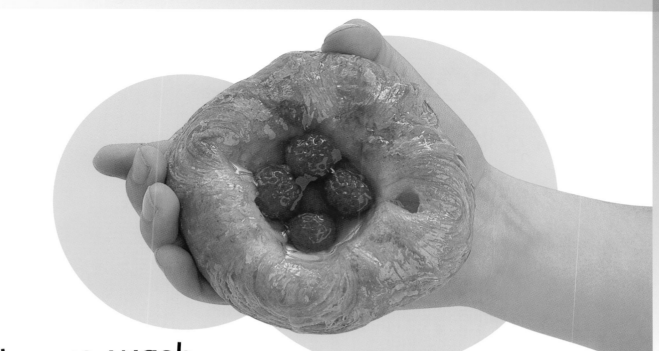

Always wash your hands before touching food.

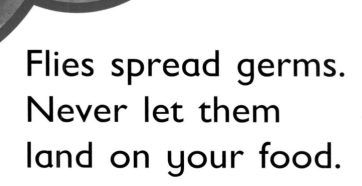

Flies spread germs. Never let them land on your food.

Sun care

To be healthy,
we need to be careful
in the sun.

Wearing a T-shirt and a sunhat helps
protect our skin.

Sun lotion helps
stop our skin
from burning.

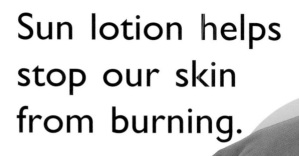

Stay in the
shade in the
middle of
the day.

Sun or shade

On a summer's day, stand in the shade
for a minute, then go out into the sun.
Do you notice any difference?

Medicines

Doctors give us medicines to make us better when we are sick.

Nice or nasty?
When was the last time you were given medicine? How did it taste?

Never take medicines on your own.

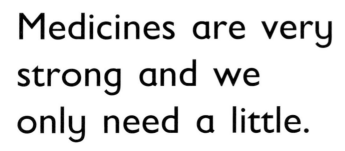

Medicines are very strong and we only need a little.

We keep medicines in a safe place.

Some medicines look like candies but they can be dangerous. Never eat them.

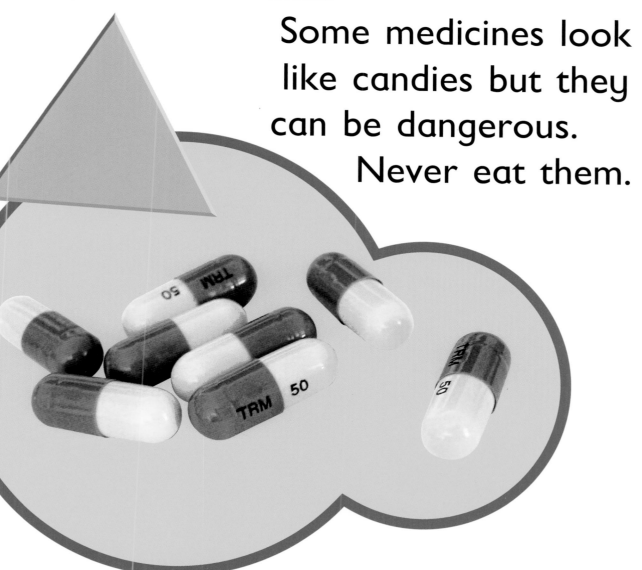

A good sleep

At the end of the day our bodies need to rest.

We sleep all night long.

Sleepy head

How do you know when you are tired?
What do you feel like doing then?

Rest and sleep
help make us
better when we
feel sick.

Sleep gives us
energy for the
day ahead.

Glossary

Appetite
wanting food because you feel hungry

Bones
the hard parts inside the body

Energy
a feeling of get-up-and-go

Exercise
activity for the body

Germs
tiny living things that spread sickness

Healthy
to be fit and well

Heart
the part of your body that pumps blood around

Lungs
the parts of the body that help you breathe

Muscles
the parts of the body that help you move

Portion
a serving of food

Make a fruit kebab

1. Choose three fruits you like to eat, for example, banana, kiwifruit, and oranges.

2. With a grown-up, wash, peel, and slice the fruit.

3. Thread the fruit onto some wooden skewers or cocktail sticks, one piece at a time. Eat and enjoy!

Index